SEX

DEPRESSION

ANIMALS

THE JOURNAL CHARLES B. WHEELER POETRY PRIZE

SEX

DEPRESSION

ANIMALS

Poems

Mag Gabbert

MAD CREEK BOOKS, AN IMPRINT OF
THE OHIO STATE UNIVERSITY PRESS
COLUMBUS

Mad Creek Books, an imprint of The Ohio State University Press.

Library of Congress Cataloging-in-Publication Data
Names: Gabbert, Mag, author.
Title: Sex depression animals : poems / Mag Gabbert.
Description: Columbus : Mad Creek Books, an imprint of The Ohio State University Press,
    [2023] | Summary: "A poetry collection that recontextualizes the traumas of the author's
    adolescence while charting new paths toward linguistic and bodily autonomy as a young
    adult"—Provided by publisher.
Identifiers: LCCN 2022038424 | ISBN 9780814258613 (paperback) | ISBN 0814258611
    (paperback) | ISBN 9780814282663 (ebook) | ISBN 0814282660 (ebook)
Subjects: LCGFT: Poetry.
Classification: LCC PS3607.A228 S49 2023 | DDC 811/.6—dc23/eng/20220909
LC record available at https://lccn.loc.gov/2022038424

Cover design by Derek Thornton
Text design by Juliet Williams
Type set in Adobe Garamond Pro

Contents

I

II

My mind now turns to speaking of bodies

that turn into new bodies.

—Ovid, *Metamorphoses*

I

Steam

tracing the obvious
curves of your shoulder blades
like wings
as you sleep beside me

I remember a friend
who recently witnessed
a man's heart transplant surgery

she said the room smelled
so clean
then after his chest
was sawed open
after the single note
strung by blade against bone
a burnt fragrance rose up
like an offering

in the language of steam
everything is a metaphor
exhaust   pressure
valve   piston   chamber

the way you turn
your feverish body
from one side to the other

last week I read
about a Chinese scientist
with the surname "He"
who had altered a set
of babies' genes
I kept thinking *He*
was a deified pronoun
as in *He who created*
you out of ashes

and since steam
is invisible
I've been thinking
about effervescence

because we call "steam"
the mist of droplets
formed as it condenses
so we only see it
when it's disappearing

I've been thinking
that transcendence must
require water and heat

last night there was
a room made of glass
at the base of a mountain
and I stood inside it
naked
wiping cloud from my cheeks

Ship

maybe we find ships
Romantic because that word is
both a noun and a verb

I once took a trip
on a cruise with an Olympic-
sized pool that floated flat
above the sea

then my grandmother
and I took a ferry to the shore
to look at gardens

her blood sugar dipped low
and she forgot what to call
the flowers or the city
we were in Oslo

she kept asking
are we doing the right thing

now her thoughts trail
behind me like
a wake
I keep on crossing

other nouns that are verbs
sink   treat   wish

maybe I want
an out-of-body experience
like hers

beam   blossom
fathom   lure

even when you and I
fall asleep holding hands
I still   *drift*   away I flotsam

I smell the stems the floating leaves
a vase of my grandmother's
even though it sits empty

and you say it's okay
to cut some things
away from their body

I'm at the edge
of a pier before morning
reeling and casting

I think

how often has the vessel
of this body
been filled up to its lip

    buoy   slip

Lake

You can't cum from behind me anymore
because, once, I said it hurt.

A plane floats outside the window,
like a fish in dark water.

I only remember how to make two things
out of paper: stars and boats.

Every morning by the time we wake up,
the day's already broken.

When my grandmother had run out
of language, I folded

a handful of stars as a gift for her, and she
just swallowed them.

Wedding

Still simmering from the last sips of champagne, we stayed in the old boat-house beside the lake and began taking down decorations—unfastening, untying, unwinding each thing we'd assembled for your sister the day before. I followed every familiar gesture, the language of long-time friends. We only had the room until dawn, and I, your date in the absence of your spouse, helped undo any pieces that could be undone. First, the tulle, once netting lavender light, gathered in ectoplasmic bouquets. Then, the discarded stems of each sparkler. With mine I'd streaked hearts as the bride stepped from the porch; you'd held the lit wand to your lips and pretended you would swallow the glow like a sun. We took the baby's breath, violets, and bluebonnets from their vases and scattered them in the lawn. We snuffed each candle out until nothing but smoke slinked toward the wood-planked ceiling. The moon poured its pale sheen, its light somehow a bright shadow. We shook the silver glitter from each tablecloth, watched the fabrics linger like water above us a moment, then let them fall to our bodies. We carried the altar out to the neighbor's truck bed. His headlights swayed to the west and diminished. No trace of ceremony left, we stepped from the airy hall to the banks of the slick, black lake. I stood, hungry, at its lip. I thought to immerse myself. I thought to push you in. The darkness began to become us.

David

after Michelangelo

I was struck by your hands—
the right one, in particular—
so massive against your neat thigh.
And your posture,
half tense and half slack.
Tracing your gaze, I think
you must be looking for someone,
or dreaming
of the impossibly long sinews
of your enemies, plucked
and strung across the open
mouths of lyres.

I am consumed
by violent stillness—

that you do not reach for me.
That you are not that kind
of man, but could have been
a wide, cool platform
to lie down on,
an empty plate for me to lick,
tracing the veined marble
with my tongue.

Blue

an abecedarian for Leila Chatti

annunciation is what we call the day when Mary conceived a son

blue has been known to belong to the gods even though it bespangles both men
and death and

cloaked in it Mary was told she'd be *blessed* at least among women

did she know yet that it was just an illusion a light-trick like on wings and
snakeskins

eyeing her hesitance the angel explained yes a shadow yes burdens but *do not be
afraid*

from the same linguistic tree as *black blade blossom blank* and *blaze*

God said *let there be* something a sky maybe an ocean and so it began

how can this happen Mary asked

in the ancient texts there was supposedly no name for it nothing written on the
parchment

just blackout breathtaken blotted bereaved bleary-eyed brief

know that *boy* comes from *boo* as in spirit and *God* means *the one who receives*

likewise women behave best when they bear babies

Mary hovered midway between the black of despair and the white brink of clarity

not unlike Eve whose name means sun falling beneath darkness

Old Norse for *lead-like* and *livid* lead into *blackish blue as if by bruising* perhaps the angel himself planted the seed before he departed perhaps Mary

questioned him asking *how* simply because she didn't know about the process

related to Old French for *pale pallid* or *ashen* in other words filled with doubt
bracing herself

supposedly B-words like breach and bundle boil down to old fears

the stranger in Mary's house drew near said *behold* God's desire is clear so what if

under his robes she only found flesh

veins perhaps bones stretched featherless across his bare chest

water which is often called a body at one point gets broken or is broken against

X marks the nameless blank space left

yes the woman bled into emptiness this cerulean chasm drained midnight abyss

zeroed out like a flat horizon or split lips a body bag left unzipped

Toilet

my first thought
while leaning over it to puke
is of a fisherman emptying buckets
of dead shrimp bait into the sea

and of the sea itself
being a receptacle for dead things
the sea itself also
a turning rotting thing

Jonah called the sea the realm
of the dead the depths of hell the belly
for thou hast cast me into the deep
I close my eyes and swallow hard

and thy floods and thy waves pass over me
the taste is salted briny
my throat textured
like the grout under my knees

once I gave a boy
a blowjob in the park
and when I looked up
his face was dark I couldn't see

the streetlamp hung behind him
like a halo
and me fluorescent Mary
running makeup running stockings
awestruck and eager
to receive

next time I spit it out
and flush
because Yeats taught me
that halos are just light nothing's
what it seems and what sucks
is my *passionate intensity*
so I give

in to the white eye its gleam
a hurricane
spun out
gaze blank and pitiless
the sea

thousands of tiny swimmers
straining
the fathom   circling
the drain
and thy floods and thy waves

Gun

Every time I try to get laid, why does
my phone think I'm about to be fired
upon? Like, "Hey, let's duck." "Duck! Hang on . . ."

Another school year has begun. The stores
have bullet-sized tampons. It's hunting season,
and yet again I'm staying out of sight.
Float, dive. You see, the best sex of my life
was with a man who just "shot blanks." I like
the game but not the risks. I like to play.

Wasn't it Dickinson who claimed her life
had once gone stiff, had been *a loaded gun*?
Do you think she meant life's a dick? If so,
what's death? What's the opposite of a man?
A woman? A wound? The devil's image?

Lace

a piece of cord used to bind or close openings / the satin corset I wore to a frat party / flimsy stitches / paper snowflakes / trimmed skirted legs / a man leaning / in whispering *do you shave everything* / the root is shared with Old French for *ribbon* or *string* / with Latin for *snare* / with English *lasso* / some men I know / still like playing games / like pickup / *linked* elbows / plastic cups / arranged in shiny bouquets / like every lip touching / so it's easy to aim / drinks all *mixed up* / eyes blackened blurry / shadows / sheets / in the 1590s to be *laced* meant beaten / or lashed as in patterns on skin / a placeholder for *feminine* / as in frilly / undone easily / *do I have to say please* / ripped panties / the seeds / of Queen Anne's Lace / eaten to prevent pregnancy / every man who's ever asked me / *do you want it* / plucked petals on a daisy / every pain I could've named / avoided / every time I said *yes* I did

Bathtub

for a while
hardly anyone touched me

      at Delphi
      no one could agree
      whether the oracle spoke
      gibberish or intelligibly

I did not have to worry
about finding orange lipstick
on my teeth or whether I was clean
shaven I did not need
to argue over the semantics
of "date" and "please"

      I count the grains
      of sand on the beach
      and measure the sea

yet tonight as I light
the pink quartz candle
next to my bathtub
as I'm silently wondering
about the size of my nipples
and the fact that I still
wear a bellybutton ring

      no one knew
      whether the male priests
      had to "interpret"
      her prophecies

I'm also wondering why lately
people always touch me
on the elevator and at parties
and bars why men always graze
my arm with their fingers
asking what each
of my tattoos "means"

>   *troubles unlooked for*
>   *shall vex thy shore*
>   *also the serpent*
>   *coming behind thee*

on my arm there's a bee
a cat with two rose-eyes
a girl wearing a bearskin
and on my finger
is a simple black compass
or the helm of a ship or
the symbol for chaos

>   *tell the emperor he no longer*
>   *has his house nor mantic bay*
>   *nor prophetic spring the water*
>   *has* drained

but which one
the men keep asking
as if it can't be all three

Constellation

sometimes people write poems
about fire that are really
about lovemaking

and sometimes people get
sunburned while swimming
because they think
they should've felt the heat

as a kid I liked to press
my hand against sheets
of paper and trace my fingers
to draw little stars

it's true that I call you
an old flame even though
I still reach
across the dark

at night when you turned on
my street I could see
the lit trail
of your cigarette sparks

you would say *let's just see*
where things lead
then my body would
become a satellite or stream

the way the sun beams
off the face of the moon
as they rotate apart

one time I curved
my hands together in arcs
and you held up your fist saying *no
this is the heart*

Gum

I used to love a boy
who wrote graffiti

loved iced tea
rooms filled with paintings

when I got sick
my mom would buy me
a butterfly cocoon
hung from a stick
cradled on another one
that looked like a wishbone

after a week or so
the butterfly would hatch
and I'd let it go

snow days
nail polish
stories
with predictable endings
like waking up from a dream
into a dream

I love knowing
that some species
of moths live off the tears
of larger animals
that no two lions
share the same
pattern of whiskers

I love the way the lion cubs
hide among the rocks
I love their whole
and heavy eyes
their bodies kneeling
at their meat

these days the boy
who wrote graffiti
is a tattoo artist

he gave me a red poppy
beneath my arm
and last week
he got married

I used to love wedding
dresses with lace sleeves

I used to want
to let a cheetah eat me
as a demonstration
of how much I loved them

I used to want to
be on a SWAT team
or be a mother
by age thirty

I used to own
a little pink
sculpture that looked
like chewed gum
it might have been
my favorite possession

I love gum
love the way it turns
beneath my tongue

Pink

first used as a common
name for houseplants

derived from the Greek
with clenched fist and Latin
to fight pierce or prick

associated with *petals women rawness*
and *deflowering* which happened
to me when I was nine hospitalized
and needed some kind of test

the young woman called *Rosaline*
who Romeo loved before he met Juliet

the word's root is shared with *poignant*
puncture punch and *repugnant*

as a child the thing I most wanted
was a canopy over my bed
a dreamy veiled curtain
to pull shut and hide in but
instead ribbons covered the beams

the finest among specimens
as in Romeo's friend Mercutio who said
nay I am the very pinck of curtesie

in verb form *to stab* or *to make holes in*

one night I unstitched
the seams of my dress and I spread
out the pieces of sparkly thin fabric
until my body's shape seemed
to go away

by 1680 the word was replacing
incarnate as the name for a shade
between *pale rosy flesh* or *blush*
and *blood* or *crimson*

technically pink isn't
a color but an illusion
we perceive by mixing the two
light spectrum extremes

I used to love getting wasted at parties
stumbling across the street
and hoping someone would find me

to see pink elephants
means to hallucinate drunkenly

I used to tell manicurists
that I'd fallen rather than admitting
I'd bitten through the skin
on my hands which I did
most days without noticing

when Romeo pleads *o teach me*
how I should forget to think

and Mercutio replies
prick love for pricking

even now when I drink
I still wake up to find my old cuts
bled all over the sheets

Crack

- One of my dad's favorite jokes starts like this: "I can't believe they got back together after all that shit!"

- Some nights he just left, and when I tried to reach him I'd hear the silence my head makes when I swallow my own spit.

- Cracked voices, codes, smiles, doors, cases, books, cans, bones, glasses, phones. Cracks taken at, slipped past. Sound of a bullet.

- Some nights I listened for tires or the slam of our screen door until morning broke in.

- *Crack*'s siblings in English, a list: *rook, grackle, castle, crow.*

- When Dad rolled down the window to hold out his cigarette, the rush of cold air always scattered my breath, like stones pressed into a nest of black ants.

- Yes, my dad smoked it.

- My friends wonder if I struggle to date men because I notice too many "faults" in them.

- Sometimes I imagine asking Dad why he went to prison (*assault with a deadly weapon; assault on family by threat; emergency call interference*). I imagine his "side" of that story.

- The punchline involves butt cheeks.

- Dad used to lay shirtless down our long hallway for weeks, yelling to me, "Smelly, come help me. Smelly! I'm dying."

- Always this space between the person we are and the person we want to be.

- Derived from the Greek *to split*; Sanskrit *knife*; Latin *void, empty*; and Old Church Slavonic *scythe*.

- You see, the nature of crack is to crack between the narrative.

- I was a kid. He always claimed he was dying. I didn't know how to help him.

- *Step in a hole, you'll break your mother's sugar bowl; step on a nail, put your father in jail.*

Sleep

I can't help but think
that every sheep finally
yields a dying sheep

Dark Matter

You hold me down   laughing
     while pressing into
  my breasts,

    say you're looking   for clusters
of white balloons
      inside a cloud.

    Then   you declare
feeling nothing,   joking
      I'm dark   and empty—

    the way my doctor said
the X-ray   should be:
     devoid   of light,   anything

    rooted, solid-seeming—
      the way shadows are
simply harmless

    imitations   of night,
while night itself is
      also nothing

    but a shadow.

Tattoo

At forty-three my uncle got one of the ocean on his foot,
which made it look like he was standing in the ocean.

But who could've imagined, once he turned forty-four,
that he'd collapse right on its shore, his chest fallen flat

as ink kept lapping against the bones attached to that
skin with its greenish-white tongues, its mouth full

of foam. And his lips, lined with sand. There's a little
black compass I have inked on my hand, a mark people

often mistake for a wedding band: a name promised,
an until-death wish, my path already set. This way

I can think about permanence as I turn toward decay.
When other awful things happen, I hear an old friend

say: *there will be an/other side* again, and yet I can't
help but wonder if both sides are the same, just this one

flipped image above and below any still water's surface
(notice the *face* in *surface,* a lake mirroring yours in it,

how it echoes *ache, ache* before the eyes blue away).
Scientists claim that humans are trained to find faces

in everything—the cracked windshield, a shirt's stain,
the stopper for the drain—but they also forget to say

soil and waves will seek themselves in our skin. Grief
involve trades: *Sorry I'm tide up. I'm knot okay.* I still

curl over my bent legs like a seashell when I think about
my dead uncle. Or fate. Then I break down to seas/ash/

hell. The pastor says, *he will always be mist.* Says, *now
he is hole again.* But even when I imagine that pink sole

of his beneath its ocean of flesh, or his branched veins
shielding their school of silver fish, they all start to spill

out from his archway. Then ribcage. I remember how,
before he went in the grave, my uncle looked like that

ocean was being siphoned up his leg, like his whole
body was turning a shade of dolphin-sea-grey. It was

as if his calf almost became a real calf then. But now
I can't seem to erase that one last image from my head.

Anniversary

There's a moment
in the videotape,
after the president
has been shot,
when Jackie crawls
onto the trunk of the car.
She moves back
toward the asphalt
five hundred yards before,
the reality that existed
six seconds ago.
She's grabbing at something—
a piece of his skull
or brain matter.
Grief, without context.
We scramble for the tools
to build it a container.
It changes shape
and color.
It moves at us in waves—
the car,
the gun,
the brain.
It's settling in.
It's eroding the shore
we're standing on.
The asphalt slips
behind and behind.
The present keeps arriving.

Bone

The day my fingers were folded into
a swinging door's hinge
and pressed there like flowers.

The way my father explained
his wife's cancer—as if it were
ice, the way his voice fractured.

In college my boyfriend's father
tried to free a horse
with hooves stuck in a cattle guard,

then it reared from the sparks,
each leg snapped like a matchstick,
and it collapsed into ashes.

Why does this swarm
of bees hang from a tree limb
like a chest without ribs?

And why do cracked ceramics,
when repaired with gold lacquer,
seem to glimmer between seams?

Somewhere the wings
of a resting monarch
close and open like eyelids.

Somewhere
a fuse
is being lit.

Somewhere a snake
slips outside of his skin
as he slips his jaw open.

Death

Felt like an empty glass.

I picked it up
and took a sip,
knowing there would be liquid.

We can't feel
when someone we love
has died
until the call telling us
they have died—
even then

I took one more sip,
forgetting.
I kept watching the show
on TV.

It was like being in the hospital
where I was born
and not knowing
I was born there.

Baby

I don't think about you
in an iridescent way.
I don't ever look
for you in the night.
I do not imagine
your endlessness.

When I think about you,
I think about myself.

And of other real things,
like dawn
on the crumpled sheet,
or the mountains.
The balance between fear
and believing in things.

You are not a wish.
You are a black and white
photo of water, hidden
somewhere in my room.

Figment

at ballet when madame said to be *weightless*

my childhood fears of being ghosted

every time I got called up to bat
in gym class and still flinched and missed

from Latin *figura* which means *shape*
or from *figmentum* meaning *fashioned*

the first time I wore blush and lipstick
and Mom exclaimed "you look so *made
up* I can hardly believe it"

the boys at recess who dismissed
fancy women as *fake*

the word's root *dheigh*
in Sanskrit becomes *body*

I used to confuse words like
consume and *consummate*

summer evenings I used to climb trees
hoping soon it would be my turn to bleed

in Gothic the same root forms *to smear*
in Old Irish it's *solid*

the clock on the steeple of my old church
had a face that warned *Night Cometh*

deceitful practices or myths

once I was sick but no one wanted
to hear it until the hospital's nurses
said they couldn't find my veins

they kept digging as I felt myself float
above the table and faces I didn't know
whispered softly "don't look it's *nothing*"

in English this root also makes *lady*
and *disfigure* and *figurine*

all week I just wanted to sleep
just sleep although strangely I didn't
realize this meant I was afraid

I knew that darkness could make
everything seem closer or else disappear

Trick

My friend John is a
magician—he covers my
body with a sheet.

Fever

I cannot make lunch today
I need a tissue
I cannot go to the store
I cannot walk the dogs
I am drained
look at me
I am bloodless
I am silver
I need a tissue
I cannot go to the show tonight
I cannot wear a sequined dress
I cannot slink across the floor
I cannot drop like coins from a purse
I cannot scatter brightly
I cannot drop off the dry cleaning
or go to the meeting
or meet up for coffee
I cannot change
I cannot make change
I need a tissue
I need a tissue
I need a tissue
they are coming out
like scarves
and then doves

June

I talk out loud
to a dead person.
The dead person says nothing.
I tell the dead person
that my tendons
are threads of pain;
my memories have grown fingers
that pull threads.
They make me float.
They keep me at home.
They make me watch
the birds out my window,
moving like smoke in the wind.

America

what does it mean
to be in love with Theodore Roosevelt
to lust for another

man wearing loose-fitted khaki
hat folded and tilted at the brim
who owns a horse unsurprisingly

named Texas
talks about how much he loved shooting
another man and says he *doubled up neatly*

as a jack rabbit
and whose own men said they would've
gone to hell with him

knowing that I have
also killed a few things
insects mostly

a squirrel once with my car at sixteen
later a field mouse and a possum
while driving across Texas like Teddy

I have always eaten meat
though I can only stomach fishing
and even then I think of the sound

thrashing
inside the red and white cooler
how it must feel

Ghost

the dictionary says "trace"

formless white latex

a plane
as it's reflected in water

echoes clearings

according to Shakespeare it is fear
distill'd almost to jelly

breath almost frozen

exoskeletons

landfills departures

remains
as in that which is missing

Hamlet said it's *a dream*

all forms moods shapes of grief

the smooth lips of a shell
when it speaks about the sea

petal-shaped leaves

thy father's spirit leaving
for rehab again

exhaust above the street

the vibration of a text never sent

every man since
then *gentlemen by heaven*
I'll make a ghost of him that lets me

the dictionary says "a remote possibility"

floating fish

the gesture of a friend

an empty ring on the bedside table
where a glass once condensed

an embryo
in the shape of a question

a bird's hollow bones

the "I" of this poem

a wish
a disturbance

"an oral game in which
each player in rotation adds a letter
the object being not to let the word end"

o that this too too solid flesh
would melt thaw and resolve itself

anything framed

anything forgotten

a dandelion
before or after strong wind

The Breakup

remembering the sensation of his hands, my spine shivers
         he   spin s
me   in   a   hive
                   and
        the sensation   i
remember   is an
   ember   in
                         pine

the manicurist paints my nails the color of pink seashells
the man   aint my   hell
  he   is   ink
      an   ail   or   pin
      manic   pain   ashe s
            in   the   sea

my dreams offer this omen: a bullet piercing a balloon
    reams of   men: a ball
      am   i   a bull   in   all
my dreams off   on
        his   pier   a   loon

I stare out the windows of my apartment like a goldfish
                do   men like
                              art
                                                           is
                 wind   old
      a   part
                    of   me   is
                                      like a
      star   i   go
            out

so then I behold this mirage: a swarm of little starlings
so   I   hold his   rage: a   little
    hen I   hold   it   in
           this   age   of
                  war   a
            rag   of
               warm   lit   tar

IV

Rat

It's the end of 2020, the Year of the Rat. My mother has finally left my stepdad, who once called my sister and me "white trash"—cheaply dressed, the offspring of a crackhead. I still struggle with (am defined by?) abandonment. I'm still told I'd be cute, except I show too much skin. On TV a woman says, *If you're about to be raped, you might save yourself by claiming you have an infectious disease.* Imagine being violated because you looked clean. Or being violated because you "deserved" it. Either way, blamed, caged. In New York, the sidewalk has split open and dropped a man into its underground pit. Imagine minding your business, then some dude breaks in. Imagine being surrounded by men whose only interest is your grimace. Pain's measurement. Imagine even the root of your name—the name you were given—meaning *to scrape, gnaw, or eat away.*

Oyster

in high school a boy
broke up with me because
I wasn't giving him
enough blowjobs

in ancient Greece
the goddess Aphrodite
made people conceive
of semen foam and shellfish
as all somehow linked

my friends and I used to play
a game where we'd make
ourselves hyperventilate
we'd stand bent over
with our hands on our knees
gasping

I like the idea
of the briny sweet slip
between the shell
and the body
between vessel and spirit

I like the pleasure
of deprivation
once someone satisfies it
for example by releasing
their hand from around my neck

I once read that oysters
are shaped by their beds
they form around
whatever they attach to

it goes without saying
that I do not
enjoy giving blowjobs
and yet I do

wear a lip-gloss called "venom"
that makes my lips swell and sting
as if someone just hit me

Pigeon

The first truck grazed him and the force
gifted him back to the air, wings splayed
seeking or accepting a current, it was celebratory,
almost, busted pillow, confetti bomb, flecks of a silver
piñata—what was the abstraction I wanted?
a cartoon's *poof,* froth of air, ineffability,
spectac—spectacular, then,
a low, fattish bullet, he met the second blow
against our windshield, each bone
condensed to one crack in the glass,
a tail-faced coin, cashed in, spent, expiring, or
inspiring, till a flick of the wipers released him, his payout
a thick spread of jam, swirl of peppermint, polish,
oil capsules, theater gel, stained glass—yes,
stained glass, a light filter, a rose lens,
oh my god, you said, *that was fucking hilarious,*
through the glaze, *that was so fucking hilarious,*
and again the flick of the wipers, a stream now
of fluid, so clear, so watery, so nourish-like, like
not blood, not like blood, not blood-like,
I could see now the absence
of sacrament, the pigeon, it was like
a pigeon, his entire actual weight, the force
of him against our motion, that collision, the fissure
he made, the tiny crack between us.

Egg

at Easter every year
we filled eggs with confetti
but first we would drain them
until each one was light
as breath when I held it

I used to find it almost funny
that we ate them
little bright
pools of beginnings
with our bacon

then we dyed the outsides
each vessel left empty
daffodil yellow
baby blue sherbet peach
mint green like a nursery

I used to wonder
whether Jesus ate meat
how his words became flesh
and why he always broke bread
saying *this is my body*

once the eggs were all dry
we would wrap them with tissue
to seal in the good news
they found the stone
rolled from the tomb

then one day at the clinic
my secrets were covered
with a paper shroud too
and I didn't feel anything
except light as confetti
in a sterile white room

but when they entered
and a nurse said breathe deeply
placed each of my feet
up on two metal rings
they did not find
the body at least
that's how it seemed

there was only the sheet
of thin butcher's paper
left underneath
why do you search
for the living

stained almost pink
with delicate petals
among the dead
or little shells

Cat

of course it was nothing
like having a baby
even though he drank formula
four times a day
and even though
I couldn't sleep

for my birthday that year
we had gone to a museum
to see an exhibit on cat deities

I once thought that if I threw him
off our balcony
it would be like we never
brought him home in your Jeep
he was light as a pile
of cigarette
ash between my knees

cat deities guarded
transitions such as
between pregnancy birth
and infancy

we were talking
about names already
you were always getting ready
to leave
while I washed and fed
and swept while he
cried out from the corner
of my dreams

he taught himself
to bury his shit and yet
twice a week
I had to unearth it

not a baby but a shadow
baby he was
constantly under my feet
scraping nests out of my hair
and empty sleeves

in the dark I could hardly
find him his dark
had started shedding
so darkly I slipped
and fell into it

Bee

I go out to get tattooed

a serpent a bear skull
it doesn't matter

I wait for the brief prick
of needle to bone

pain doesn't
ask you to think about it

a steady hum
like a swarm it swells

into heat gathered up
from each sting

simple and dazzling
it renders

me a hollow thing
a bright and present halo

Girl

an erasure of Bernhard Diensberg's "The Etymology of Modern English 'Girl': An Old Problem Reconsidered"

girl is

                    a   typical

                        generic

                            ' little brat'

                                            dog

                                urchin

                        hog

bitch

                                                          goat

                     doomed

rejected   and

           nevertheless

reduced

           short, small

           meowle

           animal

a   spiritless   fat and ugly
        bad

                                        old
plump   slovenly   prostitute

split into

                    vulgar   i   t   y

            due to the lack

Bat

once during recess my girlfriends asked
the boys to judge a *flying* beauty contest
and when they got to me one said *mouse-like
mammal* we think you're cute but not pretty

the word's root often translates to *striking*
or *disgraceful thing* as seen in *flagellum*

imagine me flailing
and flapping as the boys pinned
down my ankles and wrists and lifted
my skirt above my waist then as a prank

in Old English *bat* means *an animal that shakes*
although variants include *flicker flutter
rattle splinter* and *quake*

still I slept like a fever and rolled up the same
skirt even higher the next day because I couldn't
tell the difference between desire and rage

suggestive of witchcraft because I liked boyfriends
a movement of the eyelids who liked being possessive
slang term for explosive or equivalent to bullshit

at lunchtime we made up a game called Oreo Twist
and before pulling apart the sandwich you had
to guess which hand the cream would be in

to *lash beat* or *hit*

but I didn't know what cream meant
to be a lunatic when one boy said that he bet I had
or did *or not right in the head* so while the rest
of the class laughed my heart kicked
like a foot beneath my desk

Rabbit

The first one jumps out of my carrier,
breaks its neck. Sweetly,
the man I've been sleeping with
buys another for me.
When I set it on the bed to nap, it jumps,
too. Easy. *These rabbits must be
terribly fragile,* the man says, a new
rabbit now tucked under each sleeve.
At night, the rabbits begin nudging
against my ribcage, nesting
in the cups of my bra. They grow
and kick. I snap them, like plastic
beneath my feet. There's a rabbit
in the oven, probably asleep. The man
and I no longer speak; we lie,
hot and quiet, under separate sheets,
while rabbits crowd in beside me,
still fattening, and more start to tumble
out of the boxes, wrappers hidden
underneath the bathroom sink. One floats
in the toilet—like the others, turning
from white to pink.

Rhinoceros

I don't recommend mistaking everything for love but it's been interesting.
—Alex Dimitrov

there are wild elephants
in the country
wrote Marco Polo

    I once mistook
    the word *blubbery*
    for *blueberry*

while exploring the kingdom of Basma
now called Sumatra

    then was known for imagining
    bears bluely
    and for getting
    pregnant at sixteen

and numerous unicorns
which are very
similar actually

    before sixteen my dad
    often took me fishing
    and I always thought I felt
    the line go stiff
    then the waves would fold in
    on themselves like origami
    until nothing but a fin
    was left waving

what is the difference
between want and belief

the first time a boy told me
he loved me I was kneeling
in the shower
then it felt like it was raining

Dolphin

we like to kiss
them on vacation
flapping beneath
our life vests as we
inch toward their soft
grey beaks
which seem to funnel
us featherlessly
into blueness
suspended by sky-sea
as it churns
turning slushily
white then orange
then pink
like sherbet
like so many
sunbursts on the tongue
of a mouth that can only
taste while a second
mouth breathes

Orangutan

it's New Year's Eve
and my life is predictable
I've been to Europe a couple times
done some sightseeing
castles mainly
I have eaten grilled cheese
sandwiches and chips
flavored with sour cream
watched vampire movies
and one time I did go camping
in a teepee with my best friend
after watching the sun rise
out of the blue that morning
later on we took a bath
in a clawfoot tub
facing opposite ways
nervously laughing
every time our damp skin grazed
the other and we would say
you're not real
not real not real
which I guess was surprising
and kind of celebratory
like a sudden orangutan
too big to shield himself
with an umbrella of leaves
very Seussian-Muppety
and even extraterrestrial
or cerebral
up there in the trees

Goat

Because every man I've ever slept with has wandered off to have kids
but later fucked me again.

Because I can't seem to pick a religion.

Because, during sex-ed, my teacher showed us a little box with an open
slot on her desk, told us to write down our questions and slip them in.

Because the first note read: *Does sex really make women scream?*

Because the ancient Greek word *tragōidía,* which meant "goat song,"
somehow turned into the modern English *tragedy.*

Because my dad's nickname for me is "smelly."

Because for a long time I heard *bleat* as *bleed.*

Because *this song is sweet. It is sweet.*

Because God told his people to bring him two goats; he said they should
give one their sins and let it go, and they should slit the other's throat.

Because my brother claims he needs a new razor for "manscaping."

Because childless mothers are called nannies.

Because Jesus won't help me.

And one night, when a friend and I were fifteen, we took a late train
to a faraway party, and a man approached us, whispering, *Would you
rather be stabbed or sliced?*

Because hell is an animal with other animals inside it.

Because every choice I've made involved sacrifice.

Because I'm always the one that got away.

V

Recipe for Quiet Ferocity

Gather the following:

- At least one spotted pony on Christmas morning

- A view of the hill country

- Spotless smooth glowing skin

- Various "recognitions"

- One cauldron filled with unattached strings

- A quiet man who holds your hand while he sleeps

- An invitation to have drinks on the 52nd floor of a fishlike silver building

- The tiniest pinch of athletic ability

- A dad who isn't in prison during your high school graduation

- A grandmother who doesn't stop eating once two of her three children are dead

- Endless patience

- Immortal pets

Gather these and roll them into a ball between the palms of your hands until the ingredients condense and collapse. Become good at losing what you never had.

Acknowledgments

I would like to thank the following journals and their editors for first publishing these poems, some of which now appear in revised forms and with different titles:

1932 Quarterly: "David"
32 Poems: "Baby"
American Literary Review: "America"
Animal: A Beast of a Literary Magazine: "Orangutan"
Anomaly Literary Journal: "Egg"
Borderlands: Texas Poetry Review: "Bathtub"
Carve Magazine: "Dark Matter"
Cortland Review: "Gum"
Crab Creek Review: "Cat"
Dear Poetry Journal: "Rat"
Gigantic Sequins: "The Breakup" (all except the first section)
Guesthouse: "Toilet"
Hobart: "Rhinoceros," "Bee"
The Journal: "Lake," "Goat"
Juked: "Dolphin"
LIT Magazine: "Anniversary" (as "On the Anniversary of the Death of JFK")
Massachusetts Review: "Blue"
New Plains Review: "Pigeon" (as "Death of a Pigeon")
Paris Review Daily: "Tattoo"
Phoebe: "Sleep" (as "Trouble Sleeping")
The Pinch: "Ghost"
Pleiades: "Bat"
The Rattling Wall: "June" (as "Strawberry Moon (or June)")
Redivider: "Oyster," "Ship," "Bone"
Salamander Magazine: "Crack"
Seneca Review: "The Breakup" (first section)
Sixth Finch: "Lace"
Sonora Review: "Death" (as "Your Death Felt Like")
Southeast Review: "Pink"
Thrush Poetry Journal: "Steam"

Underblong: "Fever"
Waxwing: "Constellation"
Whiskey Island Magazine: "Rabbit" (as "Rabbit Test")
The Writer's Garret: "Wedding" (as "Your Sister's Wedding")

The poem "Gun" (as "Dear Gun") was originally featured in *Desperate Text Messages,* a zine written in collaboration with Tarfia Faizullah; "Recipe for Quiet Ferocity" was originally featured in *Fidgety Puddings,* a zine written in collaboration with Chen Chen.

I am immensely grateful to the many people and institutions who supported me throughout the making of this book. In particular, I want to thank Poetry at Round Top; Idyllwild Arts; The 92nd Street Y Unterberg Poetry Center; Trinity University; the University of California, Riverside; Texas Tech University; and each of the wonderful individuals who taught, befriended, and encouraged me in those spaces. To Jenny Browne, Andrew Porter, Tod Goldberg, Rob Roberge, Emily Rapp Black, Jill Alexander Essbaum Peng, Matthew Zapruder, Roger Reeves, Dennis Covington, Katie Cortese, Curtis Bauer, and John Poch: you all changed my life. Thank you. To Adam Deutsch and Cooper Dillon Books: thank you for publishing my first chapbook and investing in my work. To Blake Kimzey and Writing Workshops Dallas: thank you for connecting me with so many incredible writers and students. To Bruce Levy, Tim Jacobbe, and Southern Methodist University: thank you for letting me teach. There is no greater privilege.

To my friends, my marmots—especially Kait Sterling, Maggie Downs, Ariel Reno, Max Rasor, Chris McMillan, Charles Cotton, Alex Temblador, Henry Jerome Mendoza, Kenna Neitch, Amber Michiko Tayama, and Meg Brandl Tatyrek: I love you all. I would not be here without you. To the poet-friends who've also given me a community to belong to and invested time in my projects—especially Leila Chatti, Chloe Honum, Jess Smith, Sebastián Páramo, Layla Benitez-James, Daniella Toosie-Watson, Sam Herschel Wein, and Carly Joy Miller: words aren't enough to express my love and gratitude. Thank you. To my bro, Tarfia Faizullah, and my wigglytuff, Chen Chen: all my love. Thank you for putting up with me! Thank you for being my family.

To my other family, especially my siblings, Cullen, Catherine, Carina, Matthew, and Taryn: thank you for understanding and loving me. To my grammy: thank you for being a best friend and parent, for teaching me to stay curious, and for reading to me. To my mom: thank you for giving up so much for your children and showing us how to be brave and resilient. To my dad: thank you for stepping up. Thank you for getting clean. To Niffler and Bear-Lion: nobody loves anyone as much as we love each other. You are parts of my heart, forever.

I also send my deepest gratitude to the staff members and editors at The Ohio State University Press and Mad Creek Books; the time and care you've invested in this collection mean so, so much to me. And, to Kathy Fagan: thank you for choosing my poems. Any dream I might achieve in the future will be indebted to you for first fulfilling this dream.

Notes

Epigraph: This is my own translation from the Latin of the opening lines of Ovid's *Metamorphoses*.

"Lake": The opening of this piece owes its inspiration to Solmaz Sharif's wonderful poem "Vulnerability Study," which can be found in her collection *Look*.

"Blue": Some of the italicized lines quote the Bible, Luke 1:26–38; italicized text relating to the etymology of the word *blue* includes concepts drawn from *Etymonline—The Online Etymology Dictionary* and from Anatoly Liberman's *Word Origins*.

"Toilet": Lines of italicized text are borrowed from the Bible, Jonah 2:3, and from W. B. Yeats's poem "The Second Coming."

"Gun": This piece references Emily Dickinson's poem "My Life had stood—a Loaded Gun (764)" and alludes to the Bible, Genesis 1:26–27.

"Lace": I owe the initial inspiration for this poem to Kathryn Nuernberger's poems "Queen of Barren, Queen of Mean, Queen of Laced with Ire" and "Regarding Silphium, the Birth Control of the Roman Empire for 600 Years, Extincted by Careless Land Management in the Year 200 A.D.," both of which are in her brilliant collection *Rue*.

"Bathtub": Italicized lines in this poem quote the Oracle at Delphi in 560 BC (as recorded by Herodotus), in 403 BC and 401 BC (as recorded by Plutarch), and in 362 AD (as discussed by Joseph Fontenrose in *The Delphic Oracle: Its Responses and Operations, with a Catalogue of Responses*).

"Pink": Some of the italicized lines are borrowed from William Shakespeare's *Romeo and Juliet*.

"Crack": Italicized text relating to the etymology of the word *crack* draws concepts from Anatoly Liberman's *Word Origins* and Robert K. Barnhart's *The Barnhart Concise Dictionary of Etymology*. Other italicized lines are from an internet search result pertaining to my father's arrest.

"Tattoo": Written in memory of my uncle, Greg Gabbert.

"Anniversary": This poem references the assassination of President John F. Kennedy on November 22, 1963, and the recording of the event made by Abraham Zapruder.

"America": The italicized lines as well as other information pertaining to President Theodore Roosevelt come from Ken Burns's documentary series *The Roosevelts: An Intimate History* and from *Theodore Roosevelt: Letters and Speeches*, edited by Louis Auchincloss.

"Ghost": All italicized text is borrowed from William Shakespeare's *The Tragedy of Hamlet, Prince of Denmark*.

"Egg": Italicized lines are drawn from the Bible, Luke 22:19 and Luke 24:2–5.

"Rabbit": According to the *Washington Post*, an early pregnancy test in the United States—known as the "rabbit test"—involved injecting female rabbits with the urine of a potentially pregnant person, then killing the rabbits to see whether their ovaries had become enlarged.

"Rhinoceros": The italicized lines in the first and fifth stanzas are from *The Travels of Marco Polo,* translated into English by Henry Yule. In book 3, chapter 9, Polo describes an encounter with "numerous unicorns," which modern scholars believe were rhinoceroses.

"Goat": The line "*this song is sweet. It is sweet*" is borrowed from Brigit Pegeen Kelly's gorgeous and heartbreaking poem "Song." The line "hell is an animal with other animals inside it" echoes Jorge Luis Borges's description of the monster Acheron in *The Book of Imaginary Beings.* This poem also engages with the Bible, Leviticus 16:7–10.

The *Journal* Charles B. Wheeler Poetry Prize